ABC OF DRIFTWOOD AND
DRIED-FLOWER DESIGNS

ABC *of* Driftwood
and dried-flower designs

By FLORENCE M. SCHAFFER

Photography by MEL MANLEY

HEARTHSIDE PRESS, INC.
PUBLISHERS • GREAT NECK, NEW YORK 11021

to MARY PACKWOOD PRINTZ
and VIRGIE LEE CASSIDY

Contents

Foreword

It is difficult to write of this lovely work of Florence Schaffer without letting my enthusiasm run wild and dealing heavily in superlatives.

I have just had a preview of the pictures for the book and am impressed with the freshness and originality of the designs. Each arrangement is clear-cut, with no superfluous material. The hand of the artist has thinned and pruned until each element of the design has meaning.

As she is a trained artist, it is natural that design is emphasized in Mrs. Schaffer's work. This is what makes her black and white pictures so outstanding. Each reproduction is completely satisfying because of the perfection of line, balance and proportion.

Those who have seen this artist's work appreciate also the subtle color harmonies of her creations which are frequently keyed to the soft grays and browns of her beloved driftwood.

Mrs. Schaffer possesses the gift of seeing beauty in common things, roadside grasses and weeds and phantom seed-pods. She delights in the texture and line of weathered wood, building exquisite designs about such material. She also has the teacher's gift of graphic description as evidenced by the explanations and many "how-to-do-it" suggestions with which this book abounds.

Ever generous with her help as well as her arrangement materials, she has had a great influence upon the floral art of her time, being constantly in demand as a lecturer and demonstrator.

Mrs. Schaffer has dedicated her hobby to the good of humanity, all proceeds from her work being used to benefit the various philanthropies in which she is interested.

It is a pleasure to pay tribute to this gifted artist.

MARY PACKWOOD PRINTZ

Hanford, California

8

Acknowledgements (Fifth Edition)

It is truly remarkable how I found my friend Hazle Meek of Seaside, Oregon, just when I needed her most. I had never heard of her until she phoned me a few months ago. She had enjoyed my books, had several attic rooms filled with driftwood, and would, she said, be happy to send me anything I wished. Two cartons of driftwood fragments to use in miniature arrangements were followed by four larger cartons of bowls, vases, etc. They were appreciated so much because I was at work revising and enlarging the *ABC of Driftwood*, in preparation for a fifth edition, and I needed lots of new driftwood pieces. So, to Hazle Meek, my profuse thanks and gratitude!

Since dried materials are natural companions for weathered wood, we added a chapter on the subject. My top scroungers were Evonne Martin and Yonki Hamada who brought me many choice materials including pampas grass and Japanese persimmon in clusters. Verna Pearson gave me free access to her extensive garden which I was allowed to raid even when she was not there. I am grateful also to the David Ostroms, the J. D. Roberts, and the Bert Blooms for helping me with plants such as okra, papyrus heads and palm fronds.

Bamboo containers are immensely popular, easily made, and the variety in designs is endless. Two of our grandsons, Richard and David Schaffer, cut down the forty and fifty foot bamboo stalks, later sawing them into the correct lengths for planters and vases. There seems to be no generation gaps between us!

Ever faithful Mary Packwood, who helps correct and edit what I have written, is indispensable as she also types the finished work.

Mel Manley, who did most of the photography for two of my books, was once again faithfully on the job. He is even getting interested in flower arrangement!

Many others have assisted with encouragement and suggestions; my heartfelt appreciation to all.

Florence M. Schaffer

SPRING 1971

Acknowledgments

So many had a part in bringing this book into being that it is impossible to mention all of them by name.

The first little book I published (1955) featuring driftwood arrangements was dedicated to my husband, with these words, "To Chas. Schaffer who played second fiddle so harmoniously with hammer, rasp and saw." He has carried on in the same way through the busy year of preparation for this book. Hammer, rasp and saw as well as drills and brushes in his hands have solved many mechanical problems and saved innumerable hours.

A special word of appreciation must go to the busiest man in town who volunteered to do my typing. Grant Erickson brought order out of my scribbled script that was almost void of punctuation marks and full of misspelled words. This was a heavy burden off my shoulders for I cannot type, and writing was the least interesting phase of the work.

Very few florist flowers were used in creating these designs, for relatives, friends and neighbors were generous with their choicest blooms.

Special thanks to my sisters-in-law, Lois Larson, Amelia Hammersten, Anne Young and Helen Schaffer for the privilege of raiding their gardens. Likewise to friends and neighbors Zillah Williams, Ellen Scheline, Ruby Rouch, and Esther Johnson, Olivia Peterson, and the Wilcox brothers, Bill and Al. And to Clara Streit, Vi Seimandi and Eva Hill of Fresno who brought me loads of flowers and loaned me some of their choicest wood forms.

Mel Manley's photography speaks for itself. But a few words are due him for the patient, kindly manner he always maintained while I set up and checked every arrangement before he took the pictures. I can only hope he feels as kindly toward me as I do toward him.

Virgie Lee Cassidy has had the role of encouraging my sometimes wavering morale, making invaluable suggestions as we worked together gathering driftwood, cleaning, painting, trimming and setting up arrangements. A kindred spirit indeed!

I am equally indebted to Mary Packwood Printz of Hanford. She has proofread all script and suggested changes to clarify meanings as she studied each illustration with its accompanying how-to-do-it instructions. Her sympathetic understanding of all the problems involved was invaluable to me.

Practical Techniques

Growing and arranging flowers were my hobbies for 40 years before driftwood diverted me fourteen years ago. Interest in wood forms began when I started looking for curved graceful pieces that had a silvery patina and were the right size to use in arrangements. All wood that did not answer the above description was cast aside. It was a couple of years before I realized what treasures I had abandoned, and that form, texture and finish could be changed almost at will if one had the imagination and physical stamina to wield a few tools. When one is impelled by an inner urge, physical strength can be at a fairly low ebb, and still one's goal is attained in the "little by little" manner.

About twelve years ago I entered an arrangement using driftwood for the first time in a competitive show and won first prize. Some loved it, some frowned, and some were highly indignant that a small composition using five Golden Emblem roses, two twigs of dwarf copper maple and a piece of silvery wood in a hand-hammered copper bowl should receive first honors when the rooms were full of lush arrangements using dozens of roses, glads, snaps or other choice garden flowers. About six brave souls used wood in their entries that day. Today in the same show an entire section is devoted to driftwood, with hundreds of entries. I cite this to show the trend of the times and the growing interest of an increasingly large number of people in wood forms.

One needs to look back only twelve or fifteen years to view the very beginning of the driftwood "craze." Most of the people I have contacted (in person or by mail) have been at it, on an average, for about four or five years.

It is difficult to describe, but easy to understand, the feeling of kinship that springs up without effort among gardeners, flower-arrangers and driftwood hobbyists. The exchange of information, materials and ideas among such kindred souls is spontaneous and has done much to further these hobbies.

Many books give excellent instruction in flower-arranging, but I have not found a how-to-do-it book on driftwood. This one is devoted to the methods, techniques and mechanics I have evolved. Some of my methods are crude and without doubt there will be better ways in the future, for I feel that the hobby has barely begun its ascent in popularity. Many new and charming ways of using wood forms will be found for it seems unlikely that those who are now playing with wood and loving every minute of it, will willingly give it up. From my viewpoint, as a lecturer and demonstrator on the subject, new recruits are coming into the ranks in ever increasing numbers. There are many thrills to be derived from it. Anticipating a trip to the coast, lake, river-bed, desert or forest can be a thrill. Finding a likely piece of wood can be a second thrill. Creating a pleasing picture with what one has found can be the climax. Entering one's creation in a show is probably "anti-climax," but still a thrill. The final reward—though not an important one to a real artist—might be the receiving of a prize.

Just learning about wood can lead to another phase of this hobby. I was bothered many times when I picked up wood I could not identify. I had long been familiar with most of the living trees and shrubs and could recognize some common things like pine, fir and cedar by their distinctive odors and grains, but I was eager to know them all. My son Brooks gave me a kit of 54 wood samples prepared by the Research Laboratory of the Timber Engineering Co. of Washington, D.C. It has helped me to satisfy my curiosity about wood. Juniper, willow and manzanita, three of my favorites, are not listed in the kit, as they are not grown for lumber, but they are as familiar to me as aspen and oak. I learned that aspen will not float, so when I found a piece of cream-gray wood under water I knew it was aspen. There is nothing monotonous about the material one picks up. Variations in kind, color, texture, grain and form are endless. One is hard-put to find two pieces similar enough in tone and grain to use together, even when they are the same variety.

To make this book as practical and down-to-earth as possible, most of the how-to-do-it information is given with each illustration so that one can view the picture while reading instructions about it, without the flipping back and forth of pages.

Hobbies Within a Hobby

There are many separate hobbies within the driftwood hobby. The starting point is the same—looking for wood forms—but from there the roads diverge.

Dramatic abstract forms interest some. Color, grain and shape are all considered. Often the hobbyists in this "class" have no inclination to incorporate their wood into arrangements. Rhythm, color and form are there in satisfying quantity and quality so "why add flowers or plants?" they ask.

Looking for wood that can be fashioned into lamps is the most satisfying path for others to follow. This may seem narrow and confined to many, but astonishment and wonder grows when one beholds their creative work. The varieties and shades of wood are endless; shapes and forms are no less so.

Some are content to look for fireplace wood, the heavy, pitchy kind that burns long and beautifully with blue, green, yellow, orange or red flame. Perhaps they have something that some of us more active beavers lack. Looking into such a fire can conjure pictures and moods that start the images of the mind on paths of poetry and music.

I have an artist friend, Nick Guastella of Pacific Grove, California, who sees in a piece of driftwood the potentials of an animal or human form and proceeds with sculptor's mallet and chisels to carve out that hidden object. Polishing, staining, waxing and finishing in various ways makes his sculptured forms very lovely, and all resemblances to the original pieces are lost. He looks for wood that is solid and well dried so there will be no checks in the finished work. His work is displayed in many art galleries in the West.

Another friend, Cornelia Chase of Juniper House, San Francisco, digs juniper roots in the high Sierras. She makes no attempt to carve figures, but takes the pieces as nature formed them, and cleans and polishes them to a satiny cinnamon-brown finish, all without waxes, varnishes or stains of any kind.

Louise Hudson of Mariposa specializes in willow wood which she gathers in the lower hills of the Sierras, along the tumbling creeks and rivers. Her trays, bowls and candleholders are original and beautiful. They can hardly be anything but original, as among the hundreds of pieces she finds no two are exactly alike. The light beige-brown of willow wood is neutral enough to fit into almost any color scheme, and is especially handsome in a room that is done in the muted woodsy tones of green and brown.

Lack of storage space at home limits some to looking for tiny pieces to use in making miniature arrangements and landscapes. Exquisite bits can be found in sheltered coves, along ebbing water lines and often on uprooted trees that have been long "a-weathering."

Others use their lathes to turn out exquisitely-grained bowls, plates, trays and lamps from the burls and roots they have dug from the ground or found in forest, orchard or vineyard. Manzanita, juniper, myrtle, apple and redwood are a few of their favorite woods.

But arrangers (I dislike the word, but use it for want of a better one) can use almost anything. In some way or another it is "grist for their mill." Foregrounds, backgrounds, trays, bowls, baskets, bases, planters, wallpockets, wall plaques, candleholders, animals, abstract forms and pieces to use in dish-gardens, flower arrangements, patios and gardens are all sought by arrangers.

When and Where to Go Driftwooding

It is no exaggeration to say that old wood can be found anywhere, anytime. Orchard, woodlot, roadside, barnyard, pasture and woodpile, all are likely places when one has developed the "seeing eye" and become aware of the hidden beauty in an ordinary-looking piece of rotting wood. Some of the wood used in a beautiful and unusual St. Francis' shrine came from a redwood watering trough a half-century old. The edges had been unevenly nibbled down around the hard knots by horses that had long since departed from the scene, leaving sun and rain to weather what was left to a silvery loveliness.

Driftwood, as the word is generally used, is a misnomer. It implies that the wood has been worn smooth by wind, wave and sun. Only a small portion of the wood used by flower arrangers and driftwood hobbyists comes under this classification. A letter came from a woman in the middlewest not long ago saying it was next to impossible to find driftwood in her locality. One of the sections in her garden club's flower show called for driftwood. She found, cleaned and polished an interesting root from the orchard and won a blue ribbon in the driftwood classification. None of us are too particular as to how we use the word, not even the judges.

Learning the names of trees and flowers as well as birds and other wild life are extra bonuses that increase one's pleasure and knowledge on a driftwood hunt. One "driftwood" friend wrote me in great excitement that she had spotted and identified her two hundred and twelfth bird, the piñon jay.

Shells, rocks, cones, abandoned birds' nests, mosses, grasses and other materials for dry arrangements are some of the things of value the aware ones collect.

Seashore after Storms

Some say the best place for driftwooding is along the coast, particularly at the mouths of rivers and creeks, and, if you are first on the scene after a storm you are sure to make a "haul."

Much of the wood along the Pacific is large, and often smaller pieces have been broken as waves dashed them against the immovable stumps and logs. What one does salvage usually has a hard finish and a silvery patina that is whiter than wood found elsewhere. The salt in the water might be responsible for this. Sometimes pieces that are too heavy to move have interesting parts that can be cut off easily with axe or saw, if one remembers to be equipped for such emergencies.

In the Desert

Some prefer the desert wood that has been sand blasted and sun-bleached to a silvery gray. Since it seldom rains in the desert, anytime is the right time to go wood hunting, except during the three or four summer months when it is usually too hot. The varieties of old wood that the desert yields is truly amazing. Mesquite, ironwood, Joshua tree, desert-willow, smoke tree, sprawling juniper, piñon, the ghost wood of the cholla and other forms of cactus, are but a few that make choice specimens for one's collection.

Along Streams in Foothills and Valleys

Hunting along streams just anytime is pleasant and rewarding. This can be the easiest and most leisurely way of browsing around for wood. After floods, when debris is piled up six to eight feet high, it's a man-sized job to find anything worthwhile in the devastation, but treasures are there for the hardy, undaunted souls! Broken surfaces must be smoothed and silt removed before the rhythm of grain and form are revealed to the hard-working hobbyist. Willow and oak both weather beautifully and are plentiful in our foothills and valleys.

River Canyons

One has to be agile to clamber down the steep, rocky banks of a canyon, and often one hops from boulder to boulder to obtain some prized piece. Looking for wood here must be done when the stream is low, usually early spring before the snows melt or early fall before the rains come.

After exploring canyons a few times, one learns to look for the sheltered coves in the bends of the stream, where the wood washes in but cannot make the turn out. Here it piles up, giving the sun and rain a chance to do its cleansing work.

In the High Sierras

In the Sierras, 10,000 feet up, where there is more granite than soil, the storm-gnarled junipers are at their majestic best. Though not nearly as large as the giant Sequoias, they are comparable in age (2,000 to 3,500 years old) and many regard them as the most awe-inspiring trees in the world. They are more easily seen than the Sequoias, for often there are no other trees around them. Cinnamon-brown trunks, hurricane-twisted branches and blue-green crowns bear the marks of a thousand storms as they stand lonely and unbowed on their granite footing. In such places one can find weathered pieces of roots and stumps from trees that have been dead a century or more. For sheer beauty of color and grain they cannot be surpassed. Of course one does not see the color and grain at first sight, except with the mind's eye, but scraping, chiseling and polishing will reveal an exciting loveliness that brings a tingle through one's being and sometimes a tear to the eye. Midsummer through early fall is the best time to haunt these regions.

Shores of Man-made Lakes

Though I have searched all the above-mentioned places many times through the years and have wood that bear the special marks of mountain, desert, river and sea, most of mine has come from the shores of man-made lakes. Picture a wooded ravine that has been dammed to make a lake. Cedars, pines, and firs as well as aspen, beech, willow and oak have been cut and hauled away leaving the stumps to be covered with water as the lake rises. In my state many lakes have been formed in this manner, both for power and irrigation purposes, and I know this to be true in other regions as well. Roots and stumps are bound to come to the surface through the years. Then waves, storms and the sun aided and abetted by Father Time begin their beauty treatment. At no other place than along the shores of a man-made lake have I found so many kinds of weathered wood showing so many variations in color, grain and form. The ideal time for beachcombing is in the spring before the lakes are completely filled. Then the shores to windward are strewn with bleached wood that has been cleansed of silt and scum by the winter snows and rains.

Natural as well as man-made lakes make good prospecting territory for wood even when full. In many places one can wade in and fish out pieces of promise in both form and texture. They are heavy with water and dark in color so must go through a drying period before final judgment is passed on them. Pieces that prove unsuitable for other uses can provide one with much pleasure if one has a fireplace. What remains of a piece of wood after years in water and sun is usually heavy with resin or pitch and when burned gives off a colorful long-lasting flame with more heat than ordinary wood.

So again, I repeat, when one develops the "seeing eye," one can find beautiful wood anywhere, anytime—well, almost anywhere, anytime!

Cleaning

Practically all wood as found needs scrubbing with water and soap. If it has a weathered, silvery patina, wash gently with a soft brush. If the sun-bleached finish has been rubbed off, it can be restored by placing wood in full sun for a week or two and wetting it occasionally. A quick way is to touch up marred spots with white chalk and rub it in with the finger tips.

Occasionally one finds wood so white and clean that wiping with a damp cloth is all that is necessary. Wood forms that are found in clay soil and imbedded with gravel and dirt should be soaked in water before brushing begins.

Roots that have been freshly dug are usually so crumbly on the outside that the entire surface has to be removed. Use steel brushes (either hand or power brushes) after wetting the wood to avoid irritating dust. Coarse brushes leave the surface rough-textured, a finish which is occasionally desired. If a smoother surface is wanted, finer brushes should be used, followed by sanding with fine sandpaper to give a satiny finish.

Sometimes it is necessary to gouge out soft spots with chisels before using the brush. Much time is saved if unwanted parts of the wood are eliminated before cleaning begins.

To make a piece stand firmly in the right position, it is often necessary to cut away part of the wood at the bottom to give it a level base.

Before you start rasping and chiseling on what you have decided is the bottom of a piece, *make sure* that the bottom shouldn't be the face-side. Many times I have marred the best side of a lovely piece of wood by a hurried decision. It is difficult to erase chisel and rasp marks without a lot of extra work. And you may change your mind about what you plan to do with a particular piece, too. By holding it up and turning and tipping it this way and that, you may discover rhythm and lines you were not aware of at first. The use you will finally make of it will find you exclaiming, "This is so obviously the best way; why didn't I see it before!"

Bleaching

Cleaning all soft wood from every crack and crevice is important before bleaching. The soft wood will absorb the bleach, preventing it from getting down to the hard surface. The bleach loosens the soft part and later when it is sloughed off, the wood will have a streaked appearance. Old toothbrushes and small stiff brushes similar to bottle brushes are excellent for this job, as these can get into the smallest cracks. Laundry bleach used full strength will give the wood a yellow-beige cast. A saturated solution of oxalic acid crystals in water gives wood a pink-beige tone. A rag tied to a stick suffices for applying either. After ten minutes, wash thoroughly with brush and hot water.

Oiling

If you wish to darken wood, apply warm linseed oil to the piece after it has been thoroughly cleaned and polished. Rub oil in thoroughly for a soft, lasting sheen.

Painting

For many years I had a strong aversion to painting wood forms. I still do not do it extensively, but I have had some interesting and pleasing results in a few instances. For one of the Driftwood Teas, we used a beautiful handmade Tonkonese lace cloth with an under cover of apple-green satin. Using water-soluble paints, I mixed white, yellow, green, and black in the right proportions to make a soft, light, gray-yellow green shade. I made the paint thin and applied two coats on a piece of willow that was a combination flower bowl and candleholder. Everyone seemed to like it and compliments were profuse.

So far I haven't succumbed to using shiny paints on wood, though I have seen some unusual silhouette effects with manzanita branches that have been enameled black. Their dramatic setting made them startling and at least temporarily pleasing.

Waxing

I have used wax on very few pieces and then only sparingly. Wood should be polished as smooth as possible before wax is applied and if the first job is done thoroughly and vigorously, wax will not be needed! The best use for wax is to spread it generously on the ends of wood that will come in contact with wet soil in dish-gardens or will be immersed in water in arrangements. Though I haven't tried it yet, the new clear plastic paint may prove to be better than wax for the job of preventing water from seeping into the wood and darkening it. After working with wood for over 14 years, I have never used varnish on it. But I may find a beautiful use for varnished wood some day—who can tell? I have changed my mind slightly about paint!

Sand-blasting

I have experimented some with sand-blasting wood. A firm that sand-blasts paint from cars did a few pieces for me at two dollars each. The finish it gives the wood is soft and velvety and very effective in some settings. But to me, it seems to have taken the life out of the wood. I know that it saved many hours of hard labor, gouging, chiseling and brushing, for I purposely chose pieces that had a lot of work to be done on them. Later I sanded off the velvety finish on one piece with fine sandpaper and liked it much better.

ABC of Driftwood for Flower Arrangers

Driftwood Trays

A steel brush was used to remove the charred wood from the underside of this foot long tray. The inside had a crumbly rotten surface that was chiseled out. It was left "in the rough" with chisel marks showing, all running lengthwise like the grain of the wood. This is more effective than the picture conveys and of course less work by far than if it had been sanded down by hand. The piece of driftwood that was used for the legs was chiseled out enough so that the tray would rest firmly, and feet were rasped down so they stood solidly without rocking. For more security, one sixpenny finishing nail was driven through the tray into the "feet." Fruit of the flowering quince, plums and green Concord grapes made up this design. This tray is equally attractive from either side and can be used on a coffee table, as a centerpiece for a dining table or on a semi-partition or counter between two rooms.

This thin piece of wood came from a rotting pine tree. Chiseling and scraping out the soft wood, then brushing and sanding to a satiny finish, made a lovely, hard tray. The rim was smoothed down to a thin edge, but left irregular in shape. This tray is "finished" enough for the most elegant surroundings. A casual arrangement of three persimmons and some nandina foliage is simple enough for the rankest amateur to assemble. The tray could be used for candies, nuts or calling cards.

A manzanita slab with a weathered edge is the same red-brown color as the Indian acorn basket. Cream azaleas with salmon pink throat and blue-green low-growing juniper are a happy combination in this asymmetrical composition.

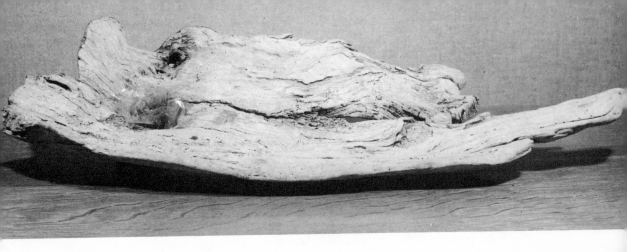

Once in a great while one finds a piece of driftwood that is ready to use without the slightest retouching, carving or polishing. This 3-foot tray was just that! The hard silvery patina so much sought after by driftwood fans covered the entire piece. A depression at the right place was large enough for a 2½-inch needle holder after a piece of polyethelene 8-inches in diameter had been pressed into hole. A natural foot under the depression held the tray at the desired angle. The design was somewhat spoiled because I asked the photographer to lower his camera so that wonderful foot would show in the picture. This made the cluster of glycerinized magnolia leaves seem higher than they actually were when one viewed the design without stooping. Squash, gourds, sunflower heads and pomegranates were two years old or more in this all-dry design. Fresh materials of all kinds would be lovely in this tray.

A tray is a tray—is a tray—but before it is a tray, it is just a rotting piece of driftwood. Cleaning, shaping and chiseling can make it a thing of beauty. A second piece of wood is used for the legs. This was flattened in spots to hold the tray steady. One finishing nail driven through the tray into the base will hold them together correctly.

Magnolia pods with bright red seeds showing, tomatoes and calamondin (a citrus fruit) in red, orange and green make a colorful display.

The second arrangement, using the same tray, is better in composition but photography fails to show the difference in color between the pale yellow limequats and the deep orange kumquats.

This piece of wood was pried loose from a rotting fir log. All soft wood was chiseled away. Next it was thoroughly brushed inside and out with power brushes. Edges were smoothed with rasps before it was sanded, first with coarse sandpaper, then finer sandpaper. Because I planned to use it for hors-d'oeuvres, crackers and cookies, the inside was given a coat of clear lacquer. It is especially nice for patio dining and always a conversation piece.

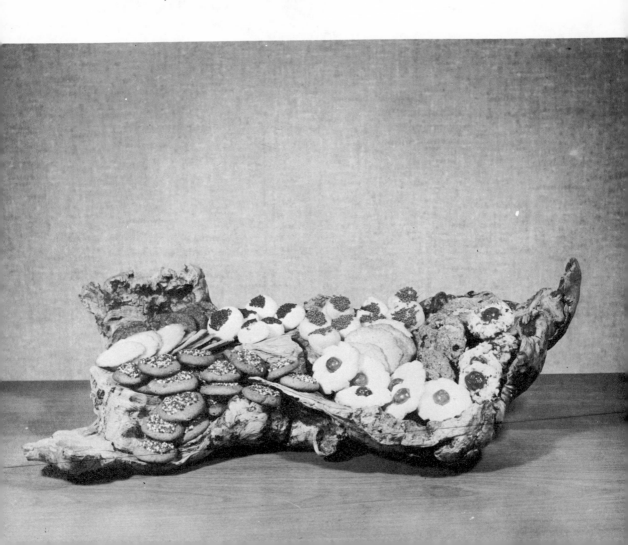

The off-white sycamore wood that was used for this tray is the same shape as when found. None of the weathered edges were touched, but most of the tray was chiseled down to 1 inch in thickness. A small piece of wood similar in color and texture was used for its base. Two finishing nails fastened the two pieces together. Pink-cheeked pomegranates with foliage made a simple uncluttered arrangement.

This tray was an unlikely piece of rotting wood, but I had been smitten with the "tray bug" so I took it home. For awhile I could imagine trays in almost everything I saw when out "driftwooding," but I feel that my period of concentration on trays has brought its reward. Pods of the day lily and golden rain tree with some glycerinized beech leaves make a lasting, lovely bouquet. A small needle holder and clay hold the materials in position.

Take an inch thick cedar board, draw a leaf on it freehand and saw it out. Leaving midrib and edge around leaf at its original thickness, carefully chisel out a depression in each half of leaf. When deep enough, sand to a satiny smoothness and wax lightly. In the back half of leaf place a piece of polyethelene, then a wet pad. Next lay lavender dahlias, buds and leaves in place.

A juniper tray four feet in length and tapering in width from 14 inches at one end to about 6 at the other is loaded with fall fruits. A few high points were chiseled out of the tray and then it was thoroughly brushed. It is as hard as flint and would take a beautiful finish if one had the time and energy it takes. Some day, maybe—my grandmother lived to be a hundred!

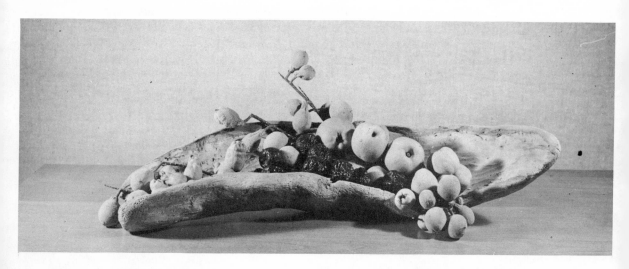

As this piece of wood was found under water, and had a fine grain and putty gray color, it was revealed as aspen. Chiseled out while still wet, it made a tray about ½ inch thick and with a silvery white outside. Buckeye, jujubes and quince are casually arranged in it.

Baskets and Bowls

How this light brown prehistoric animal got a load of garnet flori-bundas on his back is easy to explain. A disc of polyethelene was pressed into a cavity that held a half pint of water and a two-inch needle holder for the roses.

To avoid monotony where only one variety of material is employed, the design was planned to use dock in shades of pale green and beige-pink at the top working downward to dark green and dark brown shades at the bottom of composition. To further shun monotony, voids were made part of the design. The large light-brown shell of fir (16 inches long and 12 inches wide) was pried off of a fallen rotting tree. It was cleaned and rough edges shaped and smoothed with power wire brushes. Natural cavity was further chiseled out at the right place and needle holder inserted. When bottom of cavity cannot readily be chiseled flat, as in this piece, a wad of florist clay is pressed in and surface flattened to conform to shape of holder.

When the woodsy outdoor browns and greens make up the color scheme for a room or suite, this composition can be a complementary addition.

34

This tray looked too low and squatty after it had been arranged. I tried all types of bases—thick, thin, oblong, round and irregular and finally settled for the iron tripod that our local implement man had made to hold a 21-inch plow disc.

The wood is gray and beige. It was soft in some places and after this rotten wood was removed with chisel and brushes, the rough surface was restored in color by rubbing in some white chalk. It was then brushed thoroughly with a medium stiff fiber brush. Helen Traubel roses and buddleia sprays were arranged in a 3-inch hole in the wood that had been lined with a piece of polyethelene and fitted with needle holder. The length of wood is about 2½ feet.

This "half-a-log" vase has a "bottom" fitted and nailed in place. It is large enough to hold a coffee can. Yellow and white zinnias blend in color and contrast in shape with the tall spikes of goldenrod. Wood was scooped out so that shell was reduced to about an inch in thickness.

There is plenty of space in this brushed lump of wood to hold a bouquet of large flowers. Variegated dahlias in lavender and purple are 5 inches in diameter. Bouquet stands 2½ feet high. For a dry arrangement, instead of using polyethelene liner that will hold three cups of water, cavity is filled with florist clay in which stems of dried materials are thrust to hold them in the desired position.

A rotten juniper root (ie., rotten and crumbly on the outside) dug from the ground at 10,000 feet elevation was scraped and chiseled, then brushed and sanded to bring out the paisley-patterned grain of the wood. Ordinary-sized brushes were too large to get into these small swirls. Our son Charles gave me a set of electric brushes and discs about the size of dental tools that did the work well. Finishing was done by hand, using a medium-stiff brush that brought out a pleasing lustre without the use of wax.

The pink, red, yellow, and buff shades of the stately President Hoover roses blended beautifully with the ruddy-brown of the juniper.

The second picture shows cavity for water and materials, which was chiseled out of the flint-like wood and fitted with polyethelene liner and 3-inch needle holder. About a half-inch was sawed off the bottom of bowl so that it would stand firmly in desired position. Note tacks and wire in second picture. They help to hold material just where it is wanted. Though some frown on this procedure, I find it good mechanics, and am certain it has helped me win many ribbons.

A charred piece of wood, over 2 feet in length, was chiseled, scraped and brushed until it shone and was a dark brown in color. Its natural cavity was enlarged to hold an oval combination container and needle holder of lead, 6 inches long and 3½ inches wide.

This dramatic juniper bowl was first cleaned with a steel brush. Next coarse sandpaper was used. It could have been polished to a satiny smoothness by using fine sandpaper, and, of course, lots of elbow grease! The bowl part was chiseled out to hold a 2-inch needle holder. A polyethelene liner held plenty of water for the few flowers used.

Yellow cactus-dahlias tipped with bronze and a couple of sprays of the passion vine make a lovely picture in this rosy-light-brown bowl. A free form base of unpolished walnut in shades of beige and brown is screwed to the bowl, though the bowl was balanced so that it stood alone.

Shell ginger in a pale coral shade with orange-red throat was grown outdoors in Fresno, California. After seven years of tending the tender tropical plant, the owner was rewarded with seven clusters of beautiful flowers. The ginger foliage, which is a dark bluish-green, is the only other item in this arrangement.

It is agreeably astonishing how much hidden beauty can be found in a rotting log. In fact this same log yielded several bowls and trays. Space was chiseled out of this one to hold a pint-size aluminum mixing bowl. Bottom of bowl was flattened and a 3-inch pinholder was pressed on with clay. A strip of lead was nailed to back side of bowl to keep it from toppling forward.

A cupped piece of red fir bark about 18 inches long is the container for the hosackia pods in beige and green with the dark green foliage of the golden rain tree. A needle holder has been inserted in a cavity 2½ inches in diameter that has been cut in the bark. If this container is to be used for an "all dry" arrangement, needle holder can be anchored with melted candlewax. For fresh arrangement a small tin or disc of polyethelene can be pressed into bark.

This beige-gray bowl of pine was a natural—wormholes and all! It needed only to be scooped out in the center for a needle holder.

The wall flowers have lost all but the center translucent membranes of their long slender seed pods. The California Everlastings have shed their fuzzy seed and the prickly pods of the climbing chilicothe (cucumber family) have exploded and thrown their large gray-green seed far and wide. They are only phantoms now, waiting for wintry winds and rain to lay them low. The whole composition, in golden beige, has translucency and lightness.

A piece of fir bark that has been water-washed and sun-bleached is the container for this study in chartreuse, brown and gray. A hole 2½ inches in diameter and 2 inches deep was cut in the bark slightly to the back of center and a needle holder pressed into place with melted wax. Fir bark is as easily cut as balsa wood. Gray fir branches covered with chartreuse moss give the lines to this composition. Douglas fir cones in a russet brown form the background for the reversed empty cotton bolls. The stem end of the boll makes the center of the flower. Wires have been looped through the membranes in the back of "flowers," twisted firmly and covered with brown florist tape. The base is a second piece of bark, slightly darker than tray, that has been rasped at points of contact with container until it sets firmly in place. A couple of nails thrust through both pieces of bark make arrangement more secure.

There was very little to do to put this piece of beige pine into use. The charred end was rasped away and cleaned with a fiber brush, then slightly waxed, not by applying wax, but by employing a brush that had been used for polishing a waxed surface. The natural cavity was deepened to hold a 2½-inch needle holder. While working I keep needle holder handy and keep chiseling away until holder fits snugly. Sometimes I scrape lower edges of plastic or lead holders when I get tired working on the wood. A 1 × 1½-inch block 2 inches long is fastened to back of boat, making it stand better and eliminating danger of falling forward.

Bright yellow iris and foliage of the small blue winter iris are used. Foliage of yellow iris was too heavy for this 16-inch slender bowl. To make the color flow more freely through the design, pastel chalk in a deep yellow highlighted the bowl.

The center leg of this willow basket was sawed off to make the "third" leg so that it would "stand on its own." The inside of this piece of wood had to be hollowed out quite a bit. The rotting wood was 6 inches thick in places but was easily removed with chisel and mallet, though many hours were needed to put it into shape for use. Its soft beige and gray exterior and light brown interior can be used with almost any color of material. Grapes and grape leaves convey the story of a bounteous harvest. (Note the chisel marks to the right in basket.)

A piece of charred pine wood was chiseled and cleaned until its lovely grain was revealed. The burnished brown wood was lightly waxed to make a fitting container for the graceful forsythia branches. Small tin with needle holder was fitted into bowl. The deep yellow of the flowers and rich brown of the wood harmonize well with the yellow-beige wallpaper in the background.

This pine root was found imbedded in the ground with only the top
edge exposed. It was photographed as found with the tools used in
transforming it. When dirt and rotting wood were brushed off, tone of
wood changed from a dirty gray-brown to a light beige-brown with a
hard finish. Some wood had to be chiseled out of the bowl part to
make it deep enough to hold a tuna can. Pale green grapes, lavender
cactus dahlias and two sprays of passion vine were used in the bowl.
Its over-all length is 34 inches.

Another piece of brown and gray wood that needed very little work done on it. It was brushed clean, lined with polyethelene and ready for use. A lump of clay was flattened along the bottom to hold three 2½-inch holders. Bright pink single asters with clear yellow centers made a long-lasting arrangement. It was good-looking from either side and made an attractive table arrangement. Three slender candles of yellow or pink could have been placed on the long handle of this bowl. The bowl is also a good size and shape to use as a planter. After pressing polyethelene into place, excess material was trimmed with scissors.

Very little had to be done to this driftwood boat. A bit was whittled and rasped from the bottom so it would sit firmly at the proper angle. It had a natural depression that was slightly enlarged and made an inch deeper to hold a 2-inch ball of florist clay that was pressed into it. Stems of thistle and oats were pushed into the clay. The arrangement was completed with three glycerinized oak leaves which gave visual weight to the lower part of arrangement and helped to cover the gray clay. White chalk was rubbed on and brushed in to highlight the dull gray of the wood.

Both sides of this driftwood urn are photogenic. Puzzle—find the leg that had to be added on one side and the "patch" that had to be put in on the other side.

This urn was too "busy"! Several lumps and bumps were removed and the remaining spots filed down and sanded. A hole six inches in diameter and about the same depth was chiseled out. Three or four tacks with wires were used around the top of the opening for tying clusters of loquats in place. Avocados, grapefruit, bananas, loquats and their leaves make up this urn of abundance. This could have been displayed on an electrically run Lazy Susan as it was attractive from every side and angle.

A piece of bamboo that had been curing in the basement for several years was made into a vase by cutting out an oval piece on top and inserting a 2 × 3½ inch needle holder. No liner was necessary as bamboo was watertight. To make vase stand firmly and not "rock," it was flattened by whittling off the ridges at the joints. One stalk of fresh bamboo with leaves, two Finlandia camellias (white with bright yellow stamens), two buds and foliage in gray-green bamboo vase made a simple pleasing design.

Planters and Wallpockets

A split oak log, 2½ feet in length, taken from a tier of fireplace wood was used to make this planter. It had a hollow center which was enlarged with chisels and planted to succulents, ivy, Chinese evergreen and dracaena. Angel tears cover the soil.

A 3-foot fir planter lightened in color with oxalic acid to a rosy gray-beige had a natural depression that was deepened to hold two large caladium plants in red and green. A ridge of wood was sawed off the bottom side so the planter stood firmly.

Just a little rasping on the back side of this wind-polished planter, a nail and a loop of leather, and it was ready to hang. It is lined with a circular piece of poly-ethelene that holds a pint and a half of water. It took the red yam four weeks to grow to the size shown in the picture. A few leaves were removed to improve the composition and show more of the wood. Bright green foliage, red stems and silvery wood make a striking picture against a rough-textured beige wall.

A root with an unusual grain and texture was hollowed out to make this planter. The wood was spongy, yet tough to chisel out. I do not know what kind of wood it is. The cavity was lined with polyethelene as neither the philodendrons nor the Chinese evergreen need drainage.

Juniper wood takes on a smooth satiny polish if one will persist at the job. Its rosy cinnamon-brown color is lovely. This planter, which is 3 feet in length, has such beautiful swirling grain, I was tempted to take time out and do a "bang-up" job polishing it—could have found other .uses for it then. It would have made an outstanding container for fruits as well as flowers. It was dug out of the ground at about 9,000 feet elevation in the Sierra Nevada Mountains. To me, the high Sierra junipers are the most majestic, awe-inspiring trees in the world. Their light brown trunks against the granite mountains tower up fifty, seventy-five feet and more before there is a crown of green. The twisted and gnarled branches have taken on fantastic forms as they have struggled with high winds and deep snows through the centuries, for they are comparable in age to the giant redwoods.

Ivy, succulents and wandering Jew are growing in the planter.

A large driftwood planter like this one is almost bound to have holes in it after a 12 by 12 inch cavity has been chiseled out. The schefflera is a tropical plant that needs no drainage, so a heavy polyethelene liner that will last for years is ideal. The schefflera likes the shade and is a rapid grower. It doubled its height in six months. It stood 3½ feet tall when this picture was taken.

Wild grasses and mosses from a mountain meadow are planted around the lodge pole pine in this weathered root which has all the woodsy shades of gray and brown in it. The planter was chiseled out to a depth of five inches so pine has ample room to grow. The hand-carved deer is contentedly munching grass but is keeping an eye on the camera man. Planter is about 2½ feet long and 20 inches wide.

After this hollow "boot" of fir root had been brushed clean of the scaly rotting lamina, a beautiful grain showed through in the wood. It was rather dark in color so a saturated solution of oxalic acid was applied, then rinsed clean. While it was still wet, stiff fiber brushes were used to further "bring out" the grain in the wood. The pinkish-brown cast of the wood is a rich and pleasing combination with the pink begonias. For a pocket of this type a casually thrown together arrangement gives the impression flowers are actually growing in the planter.

A fallen rotting fir tree about 200 yards from our mountain cabin had intrigued me for several years. I often paused by it and wondered how I could saw out the part that had the lovely grain showing through its crumbly exterior. With only a fraction of the effort I expected to expend, I sawed through the thin shell and dragged home the forty pound piece. With a steel wire hand brush, enough rotted material was cleaned off to assure me of its hidden beauty. Chisel, mallet and saw were then used to cut and shape it. Then power brushes were employed—a coarse one first, then a finer one, and lastly a fiber brush for finishing. Although the piece was hollow, chiseling had to be done. A platform or floor was fitted in. Nails placed at an angle were hammered through the floor sinking into the fir far enough to hold it firmly, but not so far as to show on the face side. This completed vase or planter weighs 8 pounds and stands 20 inches high. Picture shows a potted dieffenbachia placed on the "floor." For a dry arrangement a large needle holder is placed on the floor and for an arrangement of fresh materials a two pound coffee can may be used.

A hollow log was hollowed out still more with chisel and mallet to hold this Chinese evergreen. (Note blooms to the left.) A polyethelene liner was used as this plant needs no drainage. The "log" is brown, beige and silver-gray.

Yellow chrysanthemums fill this beautifully-grained, golden-brown wallpocket. The ample interior is lined with polyethelene and holds a pint of water. The arrangement looks flat, as the photography fails to show its irregular outline and the voids made by placing some of the "mums" close to the container while others extend out from it. This piece has possibilities as a planter for orchids, philodendrons, ivy, etc.

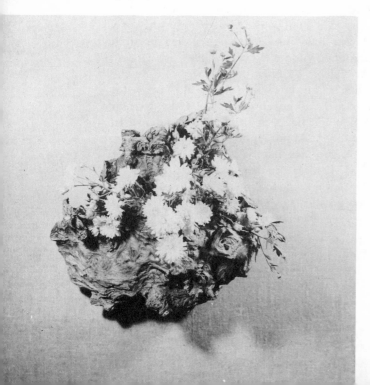

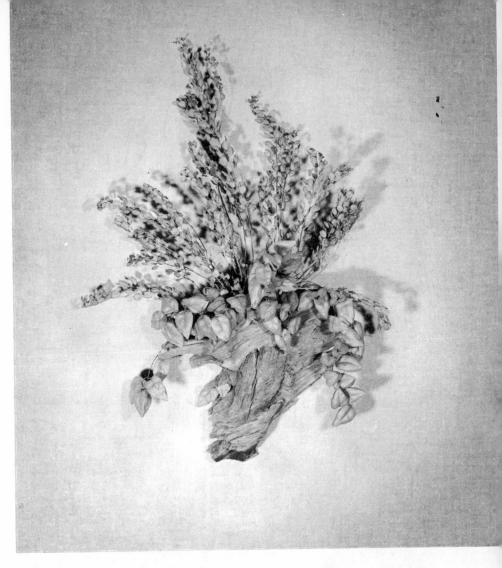

A rotting fir log produced this light brown wall pocket. It would have been impossible to whittle out the inside of this knot as it was brittle and full of pitch, but fire had burned it out, leaving it hollow. The loose crumbly wood was removed with a steel brush and the charred inside surface scraped clean. A nail, a loop of cord and a picture hook were used to make it hang on the wall. The pods of the golden rain tree were picked when they were still a soft chartreuse green. The penny cress pods are light beige and same shade of green as golden rain pods.

Lines and Patterns

Emperor daffodils had been planted by the steps of our mountain cabin many years ago. Only once until this past May had we been up to the cabin early enough to see them bloom. The rusty-brown catkins of the aspen trees were bursting into bloom and the yellow-green of new foliage beginning to show. A harmonious symphony of mass, color and line was created using a chartreuse pottery bowl, overlaid with brown, one aspen branch and nine daffodils with foliage. Rusty-brown rocks covered the needle holder.

Pink mums and pale-green meadow grass are arranged behind this piece of gray wood. The second picture shows back side of wood. A tin lid was nailed to it and needle holder secured on it with clay for a dry arrangement (note chisel marks where wood was removed to make room for lid and holder). A small can fitted with holder was placed on lid for the fresh flowers. Weight of needle holder and materials holds driftwood in position. Cleaning with a steel brush removed loose wood and brought out grain and line.

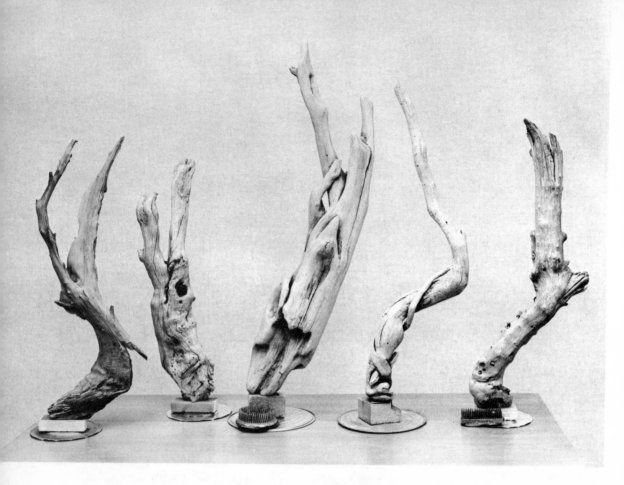

When giving demonstrations one of the questions most frequently asked me is, "How can you keep water from seeping into the wood and darkening it, thus spoiling the color harmony of the design?"

By waxing the bottom end of the wood with floor or car wax, then nailing a block of wood onto it, darkening of the driftwood by seepage is overcome. The block should be slightly thicker than the depth of the water in the bowl one plans to use. Wood should be held at the desired angle for the design in mind, then cut or rasped to fit the block before wax is applied. If the wood is very hard it may split if nail and hammer are used. The better method is to drill a hole through the block and into the piece of wood first; then either nail or screw may be used to fasten them together.

Another question is, "How can you make a piece of driftwood stay 'put' in an arrangement?"

To keep the wood from "toppling" a tin lid is nailed to the bottom of the block. This acts as a flange. I use lids from 2 to 6 inches in diameter depending upon the size of the wood. A roll of florist's clay under the lid helps to keep it in place. Needle holders placed on the flange give double insurance against tipping.

An odd-shaped piece of silvery wood was sawed oิ at an angle to give a graceful curve to the design, then nailed to the driftwood base. The vertical piece of wood was lightened with brushed-in white chalk to make it agree in color with the base. Dock and dried water lilies, all in brown, were brightened by the chartreuse dried water lily leaves.

Even duck eggs need a "cooling off" period. A plastic mallard sits calmly on her nest of sticks and grass alert for enemies that might be whetting their appetites for half-incubated duck eggs. Base is a slab of redwood root with weathered edge that simulates a shoreline. Pullet eggs painted a pale blue-green with poster paint look authentic. A silvery aspen branch with soft green penny-cress pods and velvety brown cattails with their foliage form a marshy background. This arrangement would be appropriate for a sportsmen's buffet supper.

The berries of California's densest shade tree, the umbrella, are strictly a nuisance. Just the same, the leafless trees silhouetted against the winter sky make a lovely picture. Berries and tray are beige while stems and lotus pods are dark brown. Design was simplified by taking off more than half of the berries.

The abandoned nest made secure by former tenants between two short prongs of a weathered manzanita branch has a "For Rent" sign of driftwood. Sweetheart roses, blue cornflowers and wild oats are ar-arranged in a myrtlewood bowl.

The reflection in the glass top of the table makes the lower part of the arrangement seem too narrow. This was not apparent when one viewed the arrangement itself.

A hollowed-out log with a cavernous interior can have a similar sign, signed by "Papa Fox," with appropriate shrubs, trees and rocks incorporated into the composition.

A goose girl hand-sculptured from pink Colorado alabaster by Dr. Mildred Groesbeck of Porterville, California is the center of attention in this composition. Several red branches of flowering manzanita, heavily pruned to give the design line and a restrained character are kept fresh in a small tin with holder. The delicate pale pink umbels of drooping flowers match the alabaster in color. A soft gray-green hand-made pottery bowl is flecked with maroon that ties in with the red branches and gray-green foliage.

A handsome cedar root, rosy-brown in color, was dug out of the ground near Waldport, Oregon. The loose, crumbly surface was removed with steel brushes, then the root was sanded with medium-coarse sandpaper and brushed again with fiber brushes until it shone like copper. It was sawed off slightly on the bottom so that it stood alone securely.

The translucent pods of the wild snapdragon (mimulus) emerge from a pinholder on the back side. Three glycerinized leaves of the aralia give visual weight to the lower part of the composition—both because of their size and dark-brown color.

"Come and dance with me," says this swirling piece of brown driftwood to the shell-pink oleander blossoms. Grace and harmony are the characteristics of this dancing couple and the polished walnut base is the proper floor on which to perform! Wood was used as found except for a vigorous brushing. It was then fastened to base with a dowel. Two small tins fitted with needle holders were used—one in front of wood and one on the back side. Arrangement is about 17 inches tall.

The pewter-gray driftwood sets the line pattern for the brown hibiscus pods to follow. Soft gray-green mullein leaves (partly dry and gently rolled on a finger) are the only other material used. The driftwood base in same pewter-gray is screwed to upright so that all stands firm and serene. Carpet tacks hammered into base so that heads extend over edges of needle holders (one in front of wood and one in back) insure them against tipping.

A silvery root a foot tall fastened to block and lid flange is placed in an antique pottery pie dish of brown, burned to a deep shade with much use. Cecile Brunner roses with their own foliage and small leaved ivy make up this dainty composition. This piece was used as found except that bottom was sawed off before it was nailed to block and lid.

Another attempt to achieve the casual "thrown-in" look! Many small twigs were removed from this weathered aspen branch, but after seeing the picture, I came to the conclusion several more could have been trimmed off to advantage. A large lump of florist clay was pressed against the inside of vase where branch came in contact with it. This was all that was necessary to hold it in position. Three purple clematis blossoms with foliage and buds were arranged to make a modified Hogarth curve. The soft satiny finish of the handmade (coil method) pottery vase in pale gray with flecks of muted purple harmonized well with materials used.

The driftwood in this composition is mounted on a block of wood and tin lid. It was used as found except that a short piece was sawed from bottom so that it would stand at a pleasing angle. Gray-green meadow grass and creamy onion flowers with a few grape leaves complete the design in an off-white pottery bowl. Arrangement is about 18 inches tall.

Oops! My slip is showing! I planned to tell how occasionally I resort to melted candle wax to hold driftwood and needle holders in place. It works fine if the arrangement is a dry one. Pour melted wax (warm, not hot) into bowl to a depth of about a half-inch. Hold wood in place at angle that will give arrangement the best possible line. With free hand set needle holders in wax before it hardens. Two oblong holders 1½ by 4 inches were used here. I decided to use some copper-pink roses and 3 sprays of Crimson King maple with this graceful piece of gray wood. Oops! When water was poured into bowl, the wood rose and slipped slightly to the right—which of course spoiled the design. Experience is a wonderful teacher!

A 2-inch thick slab of black walnut in the rough is the base for this composition. A crescent-shaped piece of wood in light gray and dark brown is fastened to base with a dowel. Pods of the Java Olive and 3 stalks of mullein—all in shades of brown—make a striking, long-lasting arrangement.

This chiseled-out pine log is 14 inches tall. It is screwed to the base which consists of 2 pieces of pine wood that have been blackened with liquid shoe polish but not brushed or polished. This design needs an accessory of some kind, but rather than use something that seemed not to belong with it, it was photographed without anything. Hollowed out space in the back was ample for a 3-inch holder. Fresh material can be used if holder is secured in a tuna can with candle wax. This piece can be used horizontally for a bowl, but most of its silvery patina would then be hidden. Pale-green meadow grass and dark-brown rushes make up this conventional design.

This exquisite piece of driftwood was picked up on the shore of Bow Lake in Canada. It is hard as flint, less than ½ inch thick, and needed nothing done to its weathered silvery finish. It was equipped with block and flange, and instead of using a round lid for flange I used an oblong piece of metal that extended several inches beyond the block to the right. Two small cans, one in front of the wood and one behind, hold water and materials—Cotoneaster and geranium leaves, turned red from the frost, are the plant materials.

Red fir bark 20 inches in length and 9 inches wide (at widest point) is used as a base for this mountain scene. The piece of driftwood was rescued from the mud and scrubbed clean with stiff fiber brush and water. Three holes were dug in the soft bark to coincide with points of wood at its base. Glue was applied in the holes and wood pressed into place. Small juniper branches were wired together and inserted into hole that had been cut in bark. No water was needed as juniper branches stay fresh looking for many weeks, although they become brittle and break when handled. The deer are hand-carved and painted a soft brown.

Hardwood base and driftwood have been painted with poster paint a flat black to match the dull black ceramic bowl that is white inside. Two single pink camellias with their yellow stamens add color to the snow-white flowering peach and matching madonna.

A different method was used for holding the wood in place in this composition. I pressed cut bottom of wood into pinholder just enough to mark it with pin pricks and then holes were drilled into them. Wood was then pressed into place on needle holder. It was narrow at the base with room for only 2 rows of holes or it probably wouldn't have worked.

The most interesting features of this gray driftwood base do not show in the picture. It has several deep grooves and two knot holes worn smooth around the edges. A graceful piece of silvery wood is nailed to the base about 4 inches back on the 7 inch wide piece. Two 2½-inch light plastic pinholders are held in place by a few nails around them to insure against tipping. The tall rosy red watsonia seed spikes blend beautifully with the deep red of the Cockscomb.

Two pieces of driftwood, similarly colored (gray and beige) and textured are used in this design. The upright piece has been sawed off at the bottom so it will stand alone. The heavy oval lead container and needle holder is 6 inches long, 3½ inches wide and 2 inches deep. It is placed on the base behind the tall piece of wood. There is an opening in the wood so part of the mountain ash berries can be placed from the front side of the design. The salmon orange of the berries and dark green of the foliage make a pleasing contrast with the weathered wood.

A piece of gray and brown fir wood is mounted on a 3-inch tin lid. Two 2-inch needle holders are used, one in front of wood and one behind, to hold the chocolate-brown water lilies and gray-green meadow grass. Gray moss widens the base of the arrangement and also helps conceal the tin lid. Walnut base is finished with brown shoe polish. The fir wood was found on a rotting stump, pried off and brushed clean.

The blue-green crystal bowl which is 18 inches in diameter complements the red, orange and yellow shades in the day lilies. Silver begonia leaves with the red veins tie in with the light-gray wood. The curve of the wood determines the lines in this line-mass arrangement. In fact a piece of driftwood pleasingly curved can be of valuable assistance in designing a composition.

Geranium-red and brilliant coral floribunda roses vie with each other to find favor and harmony with the light brown wood and bowl. A power steel brush was used to remove the charred wood and bring out the beautifully curved grain before it was fastened to block and flange. A homemade stand of pine is stained a dark brown.

A jade tree planted in low, brown bowl contrasts nicely with almost-white wood. Branches of the tree were manipulated slightly so that lines would conform with wood. Succulents are growing between the brown rocks at base of tree. Wood is held in place by soil and rocks.

In an Oriental Manner

A light brown porous piece of wood hides a 3-inch tuna can that holds the simple arrangement of two branches of Louisiana smoke bush. They have been quite heavily pruned to remove surplus twigs and leaves. The 18-inch rusty plow disc is fastened to a base of walnut that has been stained with tan shoe polish. To make the disc a uniform rust color, wet all over with lemon juice and sprinkle with salt. Let stand an hour or two before wiping dry.

Though the lines and colors are pleasing, the scale isn't as good as it should be, as the leaves are large in proportion to the figures.

If water had been used directly in the disc the absorption of water by the wood would have darkened its color.

One branch of wild currant was heavily pruned to give the desired shape to this simple, uncluttered design in gray and green. The bowl is green, as are the rocks which are veined in a light gray. I had found this pottery bowl (21 inches in diameter) difficult to use effectively until I put some rocks in it. Bowls one and two inches deep are much easier to use than this, which is four inches deep. Robe and hat are in several shades of green while fan, beard and branches are gray. The sprouting foliage blends well with the other greens and its size is in very good scale with the figurine. (The scale is much better here than in the preceding illustration.)

I referred to this design as simple, which doesn't mean that it is simple to do. Shaping the branch to form the desired voids and trimming off enough leaves and small twigs to harmonize the various parts to each other is not simple. There is no better way to practice than to gather a few branches of different shrubs and trees and start to work with a pair of clippers. One or two kindred spirits working together on projects of this kind can learn much. It is the commonest fault of most of us to leave entirely too much material in our designs.

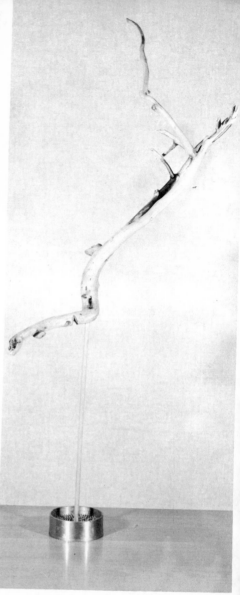

One of my ambitions is to achieve in an arrangement that careless "thrown-in" look that is so difficult to attain. This attempt shows a silvery aspen branch, one spray of gray-green bottle brush and two Peace roses. The vase, which stands 14 inches high, is gray-green flecked with mulberry. The second picture shows the mechanics employed to hold aspen branch in place. A wedge was cut out of branch so it would rest solidly on edge of vase. A hole was bored in branch to fit dowel and at correct angle for arrangement. The brass container with needle holder was for picture taking only. For arrangement a lump of clay was placed on end of dowel before it was lowered into vase.

Furled canna leaves and buds in copper tones give height and dignity to composition in a Japanese iron vase. The copper and chartreuse of the geranium leaves along with a cluster of scarlet flowers make a brilliant focal point while a weathered branch of manzanita gives the design an air of careless grace and movement.

To me this piece of driftwood is oriental in feeling so I used it in a Chinese bowl of black glass with red and gold feet. Driftwood straddles a large needle holder. Lumps of clay under wood on either side help to hold it in place as well as keep it out of water. As an extra precaution, ends of wood were waxed so water would not seep up and darken its silvery patina. Two of the purple clematis were placed in holder from the back side of driftwood and three in front of it. Wood was used as found except that bottom ends were trimmed slightly to fit better into bowl.

A cypress knee broad enough at the base to stand alone is placed on a soft gray-green wooden tray. The Chinese figure in a light coral robe that blends with the beige-pink of the cypress root is placed on a piece of styrofoam. This added height for figure was better and foam made a safe base for figurine. A lump of clay was placed on a dowel 8 inches long and thrust into the figurine through hole in bottom of it. Lower end of dowel was sharpened and pressed into foam. The styrofoam was cut out on the back side so that it would fit snugly against the cypress knee. A pink-beige palm ribbon was made pliable with water and fastened around the foam. Bittersweet blends well with the coral pinks and the steel-blue of the laurustinus berries matches the blue-black of the trim on robe and the hair of the figurine.

Three stalks of montbretia pods, one dried magnolia blossom with a rosette of glycerinized leaves and one heavily pruned maroon-brown manzanita branch in a handmade off-white pottery vase make up this "thrown-in" simple arrangement, which, for me, was not simple to achieve. The secret, I believe, lies in removing the right twigs from the manzanita branch so that the finished design will convey the movement, balance and rhythm desired. It takes hours of practice in pruning many branches to get satisfactory results.

Foregrounds and Backgrounds

Rough-textured wood in rich browns with silvery edges is the background for a hand-carved ivory bird. Dark gray slate with flecks of rust makes a substantial base for this heavy piece of wood. An electric wire brush was used to clean the wood and bring out the brown colorings. The silvery edges were retouched with white chalk thoroughly rubbed in and lightly brushed.

Two pieces of silvery-gray driftwood, alike in color and texture are used together here. No finishing was necessary; they were simply brushed and then nailed together. Pale yellow-green pods of the milkweed along with their darker green leaves give a sculptured look to this rhythmic design. The base is approximately 14" in length.

Several unnecessary protuberances were removed with a saw from the face side of this chunk of driftwood to simplify the design and make it less chaotic in appearance. The remaining voids were sanded smooth, rubbed with chalk and brushed until the scars were practically invisible. A lot of wood was chiseled away from the back side, too, so piece would not extend too far forward on a fairly narrow mantel. A small piece was sawed from the bottom to make it stand securely.

Laurel leaves make up one design while silver-tip fir is used in the other one.

Though there is ample space in the back for a 3-inch can, often evergreen branches were inserted behind the wood without benefit of water. They keep their needles, fresh look and piny fragrance for a week or more.

Mama and baby gray squirrel are playing hide and seek in a setting of silvery wood. This is real driftwood rotted out and worn down so that nothing remained but the hard resinous part. No cleaning or polishing had to be done. It is fastened to bark base with a dowel.

A honey-beige juniper root has been polished to a lovely soft sheen by using sandpaper and a light coat of wax. By nailing a tuna can to back of wood, two objectives have been reached. The can with needle holder was adequate for the two yellow sprays of golden rain tree flowers that were casually placed in it. It also helped brace the wood so it stayed in the right position.

This dark gray piece of driftwood, highlighted by silvery touches that are almost white, is 20 inches tall. It straddles a gallon-size can that has been cut down to 2½ inches in height and fitted with a large pinholder. Two of the magnolias are inserted from the front side of wood and four from the back side. This piece is a natural—it was used as found, except that black chalk was used to darken the dark areas and white chalk touched up the light areas.

This treasure was found on Pend Orielle Lake in Idaho. Its silvery-gray sheen with deeper markings makes a striking foreground for the three sprays of dogwood. A platform or "floor" was nailed to the piece on the back side. A large pottery vase that flared at the top (10 inches tall and 12 inches in diameter at top) was fitted with needle holder and placed on "floor." This piece has been used for dry arrangements as well as a foreground for planter. It once held three giant stalks of red ginger flowers with foliage—very striking!

This is the same wood as used with the white clematis. It has been reversed to show the other side. Clusters of black seed of the aralia have been arranged in a lump of gray florist clay. Black ceramic figure is against background of light beige prairie grass.

This boat with a silvery patina has been chiseled out a little deeper at its lowest point. The white clematis are lying with stems in a small pool of water. Polyethelene liner keeps it from leaking and discoloring wood.

A small thin piece of driftwood brushed to give it a sheen and to bring out the interesting grain is the background for this 6-inch Oriental figurine.

A tuna can fitted with needle holder is placed over the hole of this discarded plow disc that has been painted a dull black. A beautifully-grained almost white piece of driftwood leans against the can and covers it, becoming part of the design in this bouquet of black callas (Jack-in-the-pulpit) with their white-veined green foliage.

This sail-shaped piece of driftwood (2½ feet tall) is the background for these youngsters who have hiked into the woods for a picnic. Dark green ivy and blue-green and brown of figurines contrast pleasingly with the silvery wood. The base is an irregular shaped slab of brown cedar.

Dark gray slate that was found on a highway in the Canadian Rockies, where blasting had been done to widen the road, was used as found. Black ceramic figure contrasts with the silvery piece of driftwood found on the Oregon coast.

A piece of fir bark worn smooth by wave and wind forms the base for this arrangement. A weathered pine root, silvery-gray in color, along with a branch of blue-green juniper, make a pleasing background for the meditating philosophers. Wood was used as found except that it was brushed to bring out the grain.

A charred piece of wood that has been brushed to a burnished brown with steel brushes is the shrine for a figurine of St. Francis with bird and fawn. Succulents on a walnut base complete the simple picture.

A piece of charred wood is scraped and brushed to a burnished brown. Light-beige sea oats, glycerinized aspidistra and clematis leaves in coppery tones and beige-green pods of the horse chestnut (native of foothills in California) make up the composition. The base is a piece of driftwood finished with tan shoe polish. The cavity in the wood was enlarged somewhat and filled with florist clay to hold the dried materials.

More than once while working on this fir root I was ready to throw it in the fire! It was heavy with resin and a beautiful long-lasting fire it would have made! It had a dull, dirty-gray appearance that no brushing, scraping or sanding would eliminate. Much chiseling away of excess wood had to be done on the backside so that flowers or other materials used could be placed close enough to it to tie in with materials used in front of the piece. Fastening small blocks to the root (see illustration) to make it stand well-balanced and at a pleasing angle was no small task. Most wood is at its best as nature and the elements have made it, but occasionally one finds a piece that can be improved by bleaching. Also one might want to change the color of the wood to blend in with a particular design one has in mind. In this instance I wanted to get rid of the dull, gray, streaked appearance that the pitch or resin gave it. Using an old paint brush I applied laundry bleach full strength. (A rag tied to a stick does just as well.) This left the wood a yellowish-beige in color. After making the arrangement of deep-yellow iris, I tried a piece of yellow pastel chalk on the wood, simply touching it lightly here and there and brushing it in thoroughly. There was then an easier flow of color through the whole composition that tied it all together. No one would have guessed that chalk had been applied, but the difference in appearance was remarkable.

A set of pastels is a must. Use them subtly so their use is not detected —on dried materials, especially pods and cones and on wood of all kinds.

This fleur-de-lis is very useful in making large arrangements quickly and easily, and it lends itself readily to all kinds of material, dry as well as fresh. The iris arrangement is almost 4 feet in height while the cotoneaster and rose arrangement is about 3½ feet tall. The cutdown gallon can with its large needle holder imbedded in candle wax is heavy enough for any material one would care to use in it. A touch of red and orange pastels could be added to the wood (subtly, remember) when autumn-colored materials are used in the arrangement. Pastel colorings are easily removed with water.

For Coffee and End Tables

Two cavities have been dug out of this 18-inch willow log which is a pleasing combination of beige and gray. Floribunda roses in shades of coral pink are easily and quickly arranged, using 2-inch needle holders. Coral pink candles placed behind arrangement would make it more festive.

The shadows under this piece of driftwood belie its silvery-white finish. Rose-edged white begonias with their dark green waxy leaves are tucked very casually into the two depressions which are lined with polyethelene, pleated at the top and fastened with thumb tacks to hold an ample amount of water. Driftwood is from Bow Lake, Canada.

Peace roses in pine bowl that was simply brushed clean and small tin added to hold the roses. A few sprays of variegated ivy give grace and lightness to an otherwise heavy piece of wood for its size. It is about 12 inches long.

An 18-inch long juniper root, cinnamon-brown inside and weathered-gray outside, was chiseled out to hold a 3-inch tin. A beige-pink palm ribbon was clipped around can so that glint of metal would not show through the Cecile Brunner foliage. Leaves of Peace rose proved too large for this design.

A full blown rose and two buds plus a few leaves are laid in the depression of this small piece of root (12 inches long) that has been lined with some polyethelene so that it will hold about one-quarter of a cup of water. The root was crumbly with rotting wood. Vigorous brushing with a steel brush brought out the grain. It is a light brown in color and blends well with the multicolor rose in shades of yellow, red and pink.

A small piece of driftwood, slightly less than a foot in length, has an unusual twist in it. One side is silvery white, the other side almost black. In the bend of the wood there is room for a small low tin that holds a 2-inch bronze dahlia and several sprays of lily turf (Liriope graminifolia) and seed pods.

When one finds a piece of driftwood so rotten and brash that it looks as though it were ready to fall to pieces, the best procedure is to bash it against the rock or ground and hope for the best, regardless of how unusual and artistic its original shape may be. If it holds together, it is likely to have a sound core. Then one is ready to proceed with chisels and brushes. I have worked for hours on pieces that have crumbled in my hands when almost finished, thus the above recommendation. The time to do the "bashing" is when wood is first picked up.

This horn of plenty proved sound after going through the test. It was brushed, cleaned and hollowed out and left in the rough with chisel marks showing. It can be used as a wall pocket as well as vertically or horizontally. The even size of the different fruits in the first picture is monotonous, but the contrast in color of the apricots and plums is good.

The horn of plenty displays three rosy-red pomegranates and a few branches of red hawthorn berries.

This driftwood boat had a natural cavity. To make it adequate for water and fresh flowers, three 1-inch holes were bored two-thirds through the wood. The rest was chiseled out until a 1½ by 2½-inch needle holder fitted into the depression after it had been lined with polyethelene.

Yellow floribunda roses edged with bright pink were used with two branches of Japanese dwarf maple, which were also tinged with rose.

When boat is used for a dry arrangement, one simply pulls out plastic liner and needle holder and fills cavity with gray florist clay.

The boat had to be rasped on the bottom to make it stand solidly.

A foot long pine root has been washed with laundry bleach to remove the surface pitch and improve the color. Natural depression was deepened with chisels. Heavy aluminum foil was laid in the bottom and tucked and crimped around the edges so it would hold enough water for the few flowers used. Pink-edged yellow pompon dahlias were arranged in a 2-inch needle holder. The two upright buds are zinnias because no dahlia buds were to be found.

A piece of oak driftwood, identified by its unmistakable grain, came to a peak about 6 inches higher than you see it in the picture. Peak was sawed off leaving a flat surface about 5 inches in diameter. This was gouged out with chisel and mallet to hold a can 3 inches deep and 3 inches in diameter. A 2½-inch needle holder was made secure in it with melted wax.

Two pink hibiscus with buds and three trailing branches of the cobaea vine were used in this design. This oak container could be arranged just as attractively from either side thus making it a free-standing arrangement. Roses, camellias, medium-sized mums or dahlias might have made a better composition than the 5- and 7-inch hibiscus.

Shell-pink roses were easily and quickly arranged in this brushed brown bowl of pine wood that shaded from a silvery-gray to a deep brown. Polyethelene, with needle holder, was used as liner.

A small tin with needle holder was placed between the two prongs of this grayish weathered wood. Violets and winter iris were picked in the garden in January after three weeks of frosty weather. Wood was brushed clean and retouched with white chalk.

Animals and Other Forms

"I don't belong at this party," says this prehistoric animal as he tries to back out! A little brushing, removal of some soft wood, and the addition of a beady orange eye and one front leg makes him "come alive."

"I'm mad at everybody!" And a red beady eye makes him look that way. Glued into a hole on the driftwood base he must stand up when he would rather lie down.

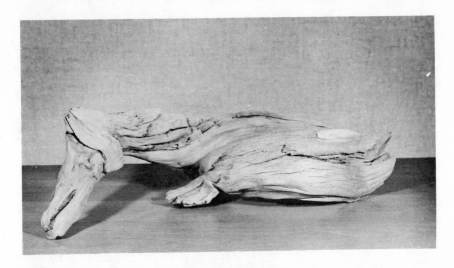

"After-the-'possum hunt." This hound-dog is resting. He was too tired to be worked on so was photographed as found. He is a foot and a half in length.

Perhaps prehistoric anteaters looked like this. Rotted wood was removed from all parts of his body with chisels. Both tail and beak were whittled down and the small dark eye backed by a paper disc of white. The wood is a light beige and has been used very effectively in arrangements many times.

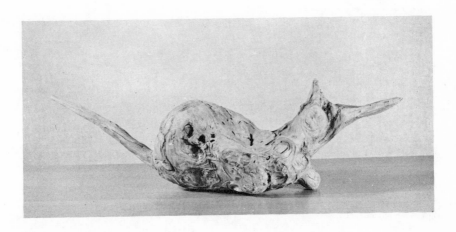

"What's for breakfast? My craw is empty," says the pelican as he scans the shore-line. A dowel fastens it to a piece of water-washed bark. A black-headed pin thrust through a red paper disc makes the eye.

With its wings spread this eager duckling calls, "Let's go for a swim."
A little brushing, the addition of a yellow bead for the eye and this
piece of wood was ready to glue into a hole carved in a driftwood base.
Photographic shadows emphasize the depth of this piece of pine root
with a hard, silvery patina. A restrained use of dried materials that
would follow the graceful lines of the wood is indicated.

Photographic shadows emphasize the depth of this piece of pine root with a hard, silvery patina. A restrained use of dried materials that would follow the graceful lines of the wood is indicated.

"Who wants to know?" seems to be the question asked by this abstract, absent-minded animal of lodgepole pine, as he turns his head haughtily. It was left on the porch of our cabin by the man who delivered the fire wood.

Texture and line vie with each other for first place in this dramatic
wood form of pine. Texture indicates it has been water soaked and
then dried. Note the rhythmic shadows cast on the base.

Take your choice, dark background or light; each has qualities in its
favor. This might be a sail boat in the China Sea and a fisherman
with his pantaloons rolled up could animate the scene.

A considerable amount of material was removed from the back side of this piece of wood so it would fit snuggly as a wall piece or on a narrow mantel. It is impressive when surrounded by potted plants or when used as a foreground for a huge bouquet, fresh or dried. It stands 2½ feet high.

"Plant me among the ladies," says this robust, "he-man" pine root, polished and groomed with steel brushes; and the ladies might well be potted plants of different kinds fluttering all about him.

It's anybody's guess what this silvery pine root represents. It stands four feet tall and would make an imposing piece of patio statuary. The weathered pine board base was found on the same day, at the same place, as the statuary (Millerton Lake on the San Joaquin River) both finished by nature and ready to be placed together.

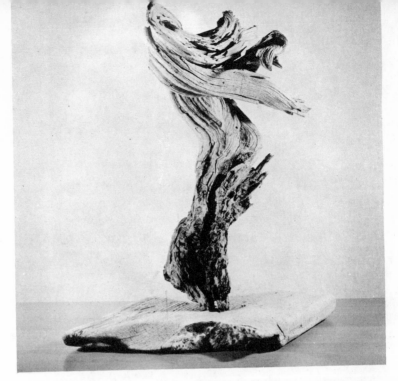

Rhythmic movement of a dancer is suggested by this piece of manzanita from the 10,000 ft. elevation in the Sierras. It shades from silvery-
gray to dark brown and is fastened with a screw to the weathered
board base.

Masts and sails of a boat come to mind when one views these pieces.
Sawing the piece in two so that none of the tips are the same height
makes for an interesting silhouette. Wood is a silvery-gray as found.

The same pieces of aspen wood are shown in the two pictures. One side is smooth and silvery white, while the other side is rough-textured and light brown in color. A bear and cubs could play peek-a-boo here.

"Cathedral" is the word that came to mind when I placed these two pieces together on the tray after sawing the piece in two. It was brushed to remove loose wood and is a light brown in color.

The texture of this wood looks like feathers, and the eye (knot) in the tallest piece and the long bill in the middle piece make one think of birds. The color is light beige tipped with gray.

Sun, rain and waves had weathered off most of the charred wood in this piece. I tried to saw it so that when the two pieces were placed on the tray there would be a pleasing curve from the tip to the low point on the left. A deer, some rocks and perhaps a low shrub could be used to complete a landscape.

This lump of weathered redwood burl has been sawed in two for book-ends. Sawed sides were polished and lacquered. Bases are covered with felt. Burl was found on the beach where it had weathered to a silvery beige.

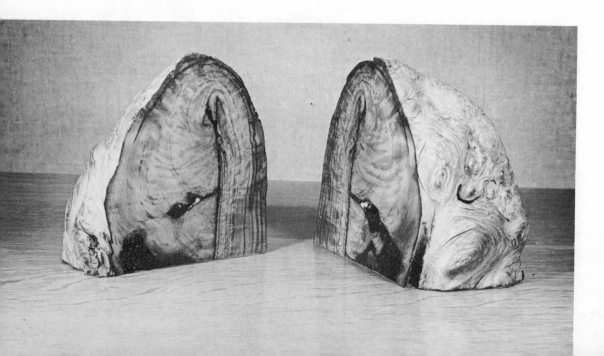

Candlelight and Driftwood

Three natural depressions were slightly widened and deepened in this dark brown manzanita bowl so that two-inch holders could be used in them. Soleil d'Or narcissus and double China lilies in cream and yellow are just right in color for the pale yellow candles that are placed in glass holders back of arrangement. Nothing was done to the flint-like wood, but if one wanted it in a lighter brown, either laundry bleach or oxalic acid would do the trick. A mantel or buffet would be enhanced with this arrangement.

A gold-trimmed black candle placed in a gold-footed black bowl makes a cheerful Christmas decoration with masses of bright red pyracantha berries and a piece of weathered mountain sage that has been touched with gold. Candle is placed in the middle of a 6-inch needle holder leaving plenty of needles in front, back and sides for securing berries and sage branch. Note that the "twists" in the sage resemble the design on candle.

As mentioned previously in the text one may find unusual wood anywhere, anytime. I was sitting at breakfast in my son Stanley's kitchen when I spied a piece of curved oak bark that had fallen from a fireplace log. It was dark gray in color so I highlighted it with ordinary white chalk which I brushed in to give a weathered look and to tie in with the white snaps and white candles that were used. The two green and white euonymus branches were wired and shaped to follow the lines of the "bowl." A gallon can was cut down to 2½ inches in height and fitted with a needle holder. It was large enough for the three candles along with flowers and greens. A rasp was used to flatten areas on the under side of the bark so that the bowl would rest firmly on the table.

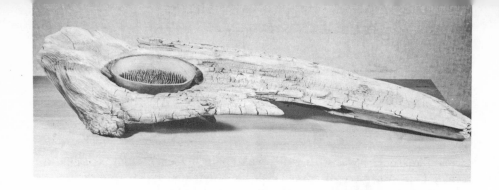

Beeswax candles in a muted orange shade make a pleasing fall picture with the brilliant orange crooknecks, orange and dark green acorn squash, deep orange pyracantha berries, gray-green guavas and salmon-yellow single spoon-petaled chrysanthemums with orange centers. The piece of pine wood is 9 inches wide at one end, tapering down to about 2 inches at the other end. It is over 2½ feet in length. A natural cavity was enlarged and shaped to hold a 6-inch oval container of lead that has needle holder embedded in it. The finish of wood is as it was found, gray-beige in color. How to make galvanized iron candle holders is described elsewhere in this chapter.

This cinnamon-brown juniper root, 12 inches in height, was cleaned with a steel brush, then sandpapered and lightly waxed. Floor wax, car wax or similar wax may be used. Tan shoe polish gave the right tone to the walnut base to make it blend with the juniper, though it was several shades darker, giving the desired visual weight to the lower part of the composition. Holes one inch deep were bored into the wood to hold the candles. The root is held securely in place with a wooden dowel. The tricky task in making this candle holder is in boring the holes for the candles and the dowel so that candles end up standing straight. Sixteen-inch off-white beeswax candles give richness and elegance to this natural candelabra.

This design was planned for a New Year's party. A 20-inch plow disc was used, painted off-white inside and old gold on the outside. A coffee can, cut down to two inches in depth, painted old gold and fitted with a needle holder, was placed under the disc. Frosty weather had turned the white edges of variegated ivy to a bright rose that blended well with the pink stock and pink "snow" that was sprayed on driftwood and candle. The two-foot handmade candle was placed in a tin of melted wax behind the hole in the disc and held in an upright position until the wax hardened. A nail was put through the branch at a point just above where it contacted the front of the can, then pushed down into the wax to hold the wood securely in place. Flowers and ivy are placed to the front of candle and wood.

The brown forsythia branches were picked in February when flower buds were swollen and ready to burst into bloom. Roses of the cedrus-deodara were bleached with oxalic acid and came out a rosy-brown that blended well with the pink-beige of the ceramic bowl. Beeswax candle and hand-made ceramic frog are a soft aqua. Edges of rose petals were delicately touched with aqua pastel chalk to tie the arrangement together. A manzanita base in rosy-brown completes the pleasing color harmony.

This juniper root, too dark in color to suit the composition planned, was brushed with oxalic acid to bleach it. (Dissolve crystals in water until solution is saturated.) Ten minutes after it was applied (with brush or rag on stick) it was washed in clear water and left to dry. A hollow place at one end of the root was further enlarged to hold a six-inch lead container with imbedded needles. Candle holders are easily made and admirably suited for beeswax candles. Cut a 2½-inch disc of thin copper and hammer it over a curved surface to make it saucer-shaped. Thrust an 8-penny nail halfway through center of disc and solder into place. Cut head from nail and file into point so that it works easily into wood. (This is Mr. Schaffer's invention—not patented!) Holes should be drilled into wood where candle holders are to be placed to avoid checks and cracking.

Let's visualize the color picture—light cinnamon-brown wood, fresh spring green saxifrage leaves, chartreuse candles and pale yellow iris against a yellow-beige wall.

Brilliant candles, carnations and satin bow in same bright shades of red indicate an arrangement for a Valentine party. Homemade candles, 3 inches in diameter, were poured into pieces of pipe from the plumbers. Candles were white, and whipped up melted wax was pressed onto the candles with the tines of a fork to give them a rough texture. (I made 8 of them 3 feet long for a wedding.) For this arrangement I cut them down so that the tallest was about two feet. I melted white wax in a long shallow pan and added bright red wax crayons until I had the desired shade. Laying them in the shallow pan, one at a time, and rolling them over quickly gave them a brilliant coat of red and perceptibly smoothed down their rough-textured look. Candles were placed behind willow boat.

Purple tapers have been dripped with orchid-colored candle wax to match the sweetpeas in this muted, pale-green container. Three cavities lined with polyethelene hold ample water for flowers and camellia foliage. Arrangement was used as a centerpiece for a tea table. A handmade ecru Tonkonese lace cloth over pale-green satin was not too elegant to use with the driftwood.

A pale yellow beeswax candle is placed in a holder that has been screwed into wood. Four pieces of wire soldered onto an iron washer and painted black make this simple homemade candle holder. A small tin for water is placed between the two prongs of the gray wood. Clusters of double China lilies, cream in color with yellow centers, are quickly and simply arranged in it.

Bamboo Containers

Bamboo, which grows a foot a day in favorable climates, has become one of the most popular of natural materials from which to make vases and planters. If there is none in your garden, see if your carpet cleaner happened to wrap the rug around a bamboo pole. As soon as you've located a supply, all you have to do is decide how long you want it, and then saw away. Or find two willing grandchildren to do it for you! In the following descriptions I've explained the techniques which were used to obtain different effects.

(*Above*) To make this boat-shaped bamboo vase, saw the ends off at an angle. They may slant either inward (as illustrated) or outward. Next, inside the joint saw down a little less than half way through the section at each end. Insert the tip of a knife where the sawing ends, tap gently and the top will fall out. Legs are two half pieces of bamboo that are the same size. To form grooves for placing these, two inches from each end saw until you have cut through the main section and split out by inserting the tip of a knife slightly and tapping to remove the two small sections. One may have to trim split surfaces with a knife or rasp so that the vase will fit on the two pieces evenly and firmly. Pink camellias are arranged in it, held in a cup needleholder secured with plastic clay.

(*Opposite*) White camellias and purple violets are arranged in a three-tiered bamboo cylinder. The bottom section had no joint so I glued a sturdy piece of cardboard onto the bottom *after* inserting a 12-ounce orange juice can into it, thus making it practical to use the three tiers.

White camellias and violets are a twosome in bamboo vases. Bamboo has been scratched with a knife to give a different effect. The taller of the two vases did not have enough space below the joint for cement, so to make it bottom-heavy a few rocks were dropped into the vase.

A piece of ironwood from the desert is screwed to a walnut base from the under-side. Both are rubbed with oil and brushed vigorously for a soft sheen. Pink camellias with foliage make a pleasing arrangement in the natural beige bamboo vases of different heights.

(*Opposite*) A dramatic piece of silvery driftwood is fastened to a redwood base from the under-side with two screws. Bamboo vases of different heights are placed behind the wood. The rosy-pink camellias with their tufts of yellow stamens make a breathtaking picture.

It has been fun making vases and planters of bamboo. Many plants grow and flourish without drainage. Several varieties of tradescantia, chlorophytum, mondo grass, Maranta and dwarf palms are among them. Anything as easy to make and maintain as a bamboo planter is a *must* if one likes growing plants about the house. Drop about one inch of charcoal bits into each compartment. Fill two-thirds full with two parts light loam and one part sand, then press plants into place and fill with more soil before watering.

Dried Designs

The world is full of many marvelous seeds, weeds, and grasses, flowers, leaves and branches to buy from the florist or to dry yourself. Their design characteristics make them exactly right for arrangement in weathered wood.

Methods of Drying

1. You can dry materials by tying them loosely and hanging them in bunches upside down in an unused closet or dry dark attic. Some will be ready in a couple of days, others in a couple of weeks. Examples: Acacia, Alfalfa, allium, dusty miller, Chinese lanterns, goldenrod, teasels, strawflowers, yarrow.

2. You can dry many plants by burying them in clean sand, or borax mixed with cornmeal. Just strip off flower leaves, put the flower heads into a box and gently sift sand (or the borax mixture) around them; continue to build up layers until the box is filled, then cover and be patient. Examples: Carnations, daisies, marigold, Queen Anne's lace, roses, salvia.

3. A good many materials will dry naturally. Gather them when they look right for your purposes. Examples: Artichokes, mullein, cones, nuts, grasses, grains, reeds, okra pods, oat (cut in late summer). Corn husks, tassels, pussy willow can be soaked in lukewarm water if you'd like to shape them, wired to bent hangers. For gourds and pomegranates: pierce holes in both ends and dry on absorbent paper, wiping away moisture as necessary.

4. Dry these upright in a jar: Cattails (pick by July 1, dip in thinned shellac); pampas grass (cut when fluffiest); eucalyptus leaves, honesty (lunaria) cut after seed pods mature, then peel off husks and seeds.

5. To delay shrinking of berries and berried branches, spray them with plastic spray or dunk them in a solution of half alcohol and half shellac, drip dry.

All the components of the arrangement are shown in the illustration used on the back flap of the book jacket. I am holding the redwood base sawn from a large burl. From the left are: three light brown stalks of sesame seed; two clusters of apple-blossom-pink bombeya flowers (although dry they hold their color for many weeks); three umbels of yellow yarrow; three dried dark green leaves of bombeya; two dried leaves of *Monstera deliciosa*; a cluster of dried kumquats (each of the 50 or more kumquats wired separately); two stalks of okra (bleached); some dried stalks of equisetum (still green in color) held together with a rubber band and pressed into a needle holder in a tin can.

I first placed the base in position and then located the piece of drift-wood centrally on the base. Sesame stalks (in needle holder with "stickum" clay on its bottom side) were placed behind the driftwood to the left; next, the equisetum, slightly to the right. The kumquat bunch was wired to the driftwood followed by the bombeya clusters that were tucked in depressions in the wood. Okra pods came next. The two to the left were wired to a protruding piece of wood. The three to the right were pressed in a crevice in the wood after I sharpened the stem to a wedge shape. The finishing touch was placing the dried foliage around the base.

Cactus spoons in orange and brown with pale green stems plus two dark green palm fronds make a bold design in this driftwood bowl.

The beauty of fragments of silvery driftwood in an Indian basket is apparent in this picture. These will be used in making miniature scenes using tiny figures, mosses, grasses etc., etc. The wood is from Hazle Meek.

Slices of birch, fastened together with nails and glue, adorn this arrangement. A pointed stick, nailed to the back of the wood, is pressed into the needle holder in the vase. Clusters of curled pods of sandalwood and Japanese pampas complete the picture.

A beige and gray bamboo vase is arranged with two russet clusters of
dry bombeya flowers, several papyrus heads, and a curly branch of
wisteria. An interesting piece of driftwood with a third cluster of
bombeya glued in a depression is pushed against the bamboo. Background
is chartreuse.

"Fishpole" bamboo which grows in patches along the river was used in this arrangement. The blades, in green and yellow, were clipped, forming an interesting pattern for the background of a piece of driftwood "planted" to some dark green succulents.

(*Opposite*) Cattails and two umbels of rich russet-brown flowers from the bombeya tree (a native of Africa) are arranged in a silvery-gray piece of driftwood from Oregon. When fresh, the flowers are a delicate apple-blossom-pink. The dry clusters hold their shape well. They will not shatter if, when they are wired and taped, the tape is brought up to cover the joints where the florets are attached to the main stem.

(*Opposite*)

Meadow-grass with cream-colored "foxtails", a cluster of wild pea-pods and woodroses from Hawaii are arranged in a low container with a needle holder which is then placed in the curve of an interesting piece of driftwood.

Brazilian star flowers in natural cream-white and dyed pale aquamarine are "planted" (with glue) in this dramatic piece of silver-gray driftwood, all anchored on a driftwood base with a couple of nails. The clumps of mondo grass, with roots, were tucked in polyethelene pockets that kept them growing as long as they were watered. Mondo grass needs no drainage.

Leftover artichokes were stuck in an unfinished driftwood bowl and left on a sunny window ledge in my workroom. The warmth further dried out the 'chokes' and loosened the fluffed seed. I was thrilled with the sight so placed the vase on a half-round of driftwood and used a cracked-open pomegranate with ruby-red seed for contrast.

(*Opposite*)
Okra and pampas arranged in a three-opening modern container.

(*Opposite*)

Gray-blue palm fronds are in pleasing contrast to the cream colored pampas and brown dried artichokes. The background is chartreuse burlap. The natural bamboo container is simple to make, just two cuts, one at the top and one at the bottom, to get the height one wants. The lower two inch section was filled with cement to make it stand more securely.

Seed heads of crepe myrtle, yarrow and cattails in a bamboo vase that is placed in a curve of driftwood. A cluster of dried pomegranates with seed still a bright red is used on the driftwood base.

A large, heavy needle holder is held firm in a natural reed basket with "stickum" clay. Artichoke seed heads in a graceful curve contrast with the stiffness of the gray-green palm fronds.

Scales of the artichokes have been removed to show the fluffy tufts that hold the seed. In the shops they are shown in many gay colors. Here they are left in their natural, creamy white which contrasts nicely with the brown cockleburs and the dark brown design on the pale gray vase. A cluster of half-dry persimmons and a bit of foliage of a miniature bamboo complete the design.

Teasel and yarrow in a dark brown handmade pottery vase. Dried materials are naturally stiff; but the driftwood gives rhythm and swing to an otherwise stiff arrangement.

Kafir corn, grown for poultry feed, is dark brown in color. Five heads were bleached to a light tan in five parts water to one part laundry bleach for half an hour. A cluster of bright orange kumquats with gray-green foliage completed this stylized arrangement in a dark brown modern container.

"Nobody loves me" is the title of this design. Japanese pampas and dark brown cockleburs are placed in a hole drilled into a charred piece of driftwood. The driftwood figure is balanced on the edge of the container and used as found.

A knot formed on a lodgepole pine tree by a parasite has been stained a light rust-brown, and then polished. Dry palm fronds, twigs of liquid-amber and the deodar roses are all a silvery gray. Materials are held in a natural depression in the knot with a lump of "stickum" clay.

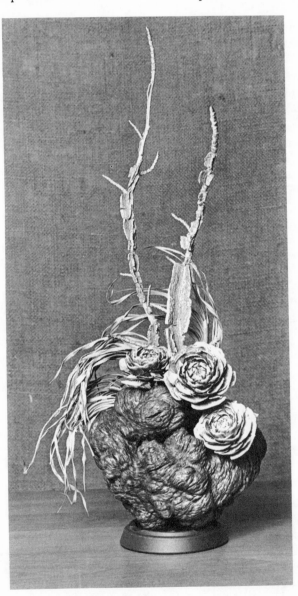

Mechanics for Dried Materials

To replace dried stems, or make the stiff ones more pliable, tape them to thin florist wires, then cover the wires with florist tape (available in white, brown, tan, and several greens). Several flowers can be taped in a cluster to one wire stem. If you need to lengthen stems, wire them to drinking straws, skewers, branches, etc. Conceal extenders with florist tape if necessary.

You can change the colors of many dried materials by giving them a bath in one part Clorox to 5 parts water.

To color pampas and other grasses place them in a plastic bag, add tempera (powdered poster paint) in desired color and, holding tight to the stems and closed end of bag, shake vigorously. Place upright in large container. Spray lightly with clear acrylic paint or hair spray. In ten minutes it is ready to use!

Use glue to put together any flowers or leaves which have shattered or broken. Or maybe some transparent tape? For heavy materials, wire and dowels may be the only solution.

I secure the pinholder to the container with "stickum" clay on the bottom side.

Some people stuff their containers with Oasis, taped down with adhesive. The dried flowers are then stuck into the Oasis, rather than in a pinholder.

Dried Flowers to Buy

You can buy assorted cones, grasses, dried berries, driftwood, moss, wheat and barley, sea oats, mullein, yarrow, eucalyptus, plumes, okra, thistle, lotus and yucca pods, acorn sprays, coconut spathes, palms, cycas, artichokes, honesty pods, strawflowers and wood roses from your local florist.

Heirloom Wreaths

Materials

Outer and inner borders: Douglas fir cones
Focal areas: Cones of piñon pine, *Sequoia gigantia,* and "roses" of *Cedrus deodar.*
Fillers: Cones of pine, spruce, cryptomeria, cypress, coast redwood, and casuarina (beefwood family). Individual scales of the araucaria pine. Beige seeds from the araucaria scales. Seed pods of jacaranda (split), liquidamber, bottle tree, eucalyptus (many varieties). Nectarine, peach and apricot pits. Nuts of the walnut, pecan, pignut, and acorn.
Backing: Thin plywood. Lining: Brown felt.
Wires: No. 18-gauge for wiring wreath to form; 24-gauge for medium materials; 30-gauge for small materials; 2 lightweight coat hangers; 9-inch brown chenille-covered wire for hanging.
White glue and clear acrylic spray

Treatment of Materials

Dry immature peaches (thinned from the trees in early spring) were dried away from bright sunlight; they retain their soft gray-green coloring which makes a nice contrast to the predominantly browns and tans of the other materials.

Apricot pits, pignuts, walnuts and pecans may be bleached in a solution of 4 parts water to 1 part chlorine laundry bleach.

Opened Jacaranda pods were dipped in a solution of green food coloring (a few drops of concentrate to a pint of water). The light borders take on a soft green tint that harmonizes well with the green piñon cones.

The edges of the cups of the red gum eucalyptus may be touched with a fine line of gold or red coloring for accent. But no coloring at all is better than too much artificial glitter. The charm of these cone and pod decorations lies in their naturalness.

Frame, Backing and Finishing

1. Cut the hooks from two coat hangers and straighten the wires. Then form into a single overlapping circle approximately 10½ inches in diameter. Wrap these wires with short strands of #18 wire. This will keep the cone wiring from slipping on the form.

2. The plywood backing to fit this form will have an outside diameter of 11¾ inches, and the center cut-out will be 8½ inches in diameter. This can be cut with a keyhole saw. At this time 12 holes should be drilled in the backing to hold the 6 wires that are to fasten the finished wreath to the backing as shown in the photo. Also drill two holes for inserting the chenille-covered wire to use as a hanger.

3. Next, outline this plywood backing with chalk on brown felt for a lining and cut along chalk lines with pinking shears. Now rub the edges of the plywood with dark-brown shoe polish so that no light area will show after the cones are in place. Plywood backing and felt can then be tied together and laid aside while you wire the cones and pods.

Wiring

The border and focal area cones as well as all of the medium-sized fillers will be wired with the medium-gauge #24 wire, while the smaller cones and pods should be wired with the finer #30 gauge. It is best to wire all materials before you start making your wreath.

1. Start wiring the Douglas fir on the stem end for the borders. Later some of these can be wired on the tips to expose the stem end when

they are used as fillers in the center of the wreath. Many cones and pods can be wired on either end, thus giving two forms to each variety.

2. To wire *Cedrus deodar,* turn the "roses" upside down in a shallow box and fill the stem end with white glue. Double a 9-inch length of wire and insert the bent end into the glue and let set for 12 hours. Liquid-amber pods can be handled the same way after filling any one of the many natural holes with glue.

3. The smallest filler cones should be inserted in groups of three or five, but they should be wired individually with fine wire.

4. Peach and apricot pits, araucaria seeds, many eucalyptus and some nuts will have to be drilled with an electric or a hand drill. Bottle tree pods and split jacaranda pods may be punched with an awl or ice pick.

Method

It is well to decide upon a general plan. If a wreath of this size is divided into thirds, the position of three focal areas of dominant materials can be decided upon before you start to work. Then filler sections between these can roughly duplicate each other.

Aim to distribute light-colored accents symmetrically for visual balance. Remembering that the wreath will be wired to the flat plywood form, keep the back flat as you work and round the materials up in a semi-circular form over the fir cone borders. The wires on these border cones should be wrapped completely around the heavy wire frame. (Or as you put in fillers over the border cones, these wires can be wrapped around another placement in the wreath.) Keep all wire ends to the back where they will be covered with the plywood backing.

After all materials are wired to the wreath form, place tie wires and chenille-covered hanger in holes drilled in the plywood backing. Slit the felt backing so that hangar may be drawn through.

Place wreath in place over plywood backing. Draw outer wires up through the cones and pods and with pliers twist the two ends together tightly on the inside and tuck in over the plywood. Turn face down and spread white glue over the backing. Press felt liner into place, drawing chenille hanger through slit. This gives a finished look to your creation as well as protecting wall or table top when in use.

Finally spray the face of the wreath with a clear acrylic spray. If this spraying is repeated once or twice a year, it will help to repel dust and freshen the wreath. To vary its appearance you may construct a halo for the wreath by stapling evergreen cuttings to a cardboard cut to the same pattern as the plywood backing. This can be hung separately behind the cones and pods. For still another variation, use the wreath as a table centerpiece with a large candle in the center.

Index